AMERICAN REVERIE

★

Synnika Lofton
&
Donnelle McGee

T°
THERA BOOKS
Turlock, California
SAY / SOMETHING

Thera Books
1819 Empress Lane
Turlock, CA 95382

www.thetherabooks.com

ISBN: 978-0-578-70393-0
Library of Congress Control Number: 2020939816

A Thera Books First Edition, July 2020

Printed in the United States of America

CONTENTS

I come up hard, awful hard
I had to win
Then start all over
And win again

—Marvin Gaye

I HAVE A LOT TO LEARN

father dear   lord
show me the journey of the sephardic jew
spain to greece to los angeles
guide me in
know i am of two ideals

mother dear   lord
cover me with optimism of my people
smiles frowns
blue green sea
cotton white fields

let me turn to   baldwin   clifton   langston
guide me
mother dear   lord
father dear   lord
i have a lot to learn

DREAMER

heavy,
like a ton of dreams
resting in a hostile environment,
like lessons that played out
in the streets
of detroit,
chicago,
new york city—they didn't pull weapons
for peace: challenged masculinity.

one morning,
my father handed me a revolver—the mississippi
heat crawled into the single-family
brick home, like an ancestor
stopping by to see what was on the stove
or to deliver the good news.

its old handle
and tarnished chrome
told stories of self-defense,
liberation:
country life for blues-people.

"it's for the animals," he said.
we were all social creatures

in states of mourning,
living,
            praying,
                        searching
                                    for a righteous
place
            to call
                        home.

BROTHER DEAD

You sat there with your head stuck in pride The choke
murder done The trembling of my hands

My wife long gone Anxiety making work of me Shadow
blurred Brother dead

Never the perfect one Let go
Daniel Pantaleo

SINGER OF AMERICAN ODYSSEY

sing as the Threat Level rises;
ow,
guarded,
elevated,
high,
SEVERE.
I hear the sirens,
sense the unique hospitality;
the violence roars
for blocks.
I fold into self:
a jungle cat, upright, fingers on the pulse
of concrete landscapes.
I'm not fearful of traffic—
only the confinement of language.
I brew resistance
in a cast iron pot.
I honor Trayvon Martin.
I celebrate the fallen.
I sing as the Threat Level
forces its way onto the skin.
I sing as the Threat Level rises.

DO WHAT YOU GOTTA DO
—*words to mother*

mother   mother where you at?
you ain't no where near here
they told me you like nina singing   *do what you gotta do*
movin' still
in the house waiting for the batta ram
knock down of the crack holding you

fade to black with whiffs into cranium
it's alright 'cause you taught me to love the rift of jimi
it's alright 'cause jimi takes body to places like
villanova junction and
i'm loving jimi when
your love is in the pipe

                    smoke fading beautifully into your scars

SANCTUARY

On this road:
Kerouac's Mexico City Blues
on my lap;
a journal smolders,
solemnly burns,
metallic sounds—shell game—ringing,
like freedom.
Everything and nothing;
God particles surface like drums
from silence.
My grandfather's hostility
stands like a monument in the back
of my mind.
Uproot *their* statues,
rip them from concrete,
crumble their sensational stories,
and cast love affairs
with history
to hungry winds.
I prefer this razor-sharp music,
an expansive temple.
Wisdom is etched on skin.

CRENSHAW SET ABLAZE

Get them weights/metal plates
Off my chest
No spotter though

I come from concrete/hands
Wedged between black thighs

I come from walks at dusk
Here along Crenshaw
Where tracks stretch long
On arms of some folks on my block

But they stand for me
Greeting me with chiseled torso
Body
A canvas of colors
Tatted for life

Like—

> one crip dead
> two crips dead
> one blood shot
> one blood confined to a wheelchair

As I watch the bullet exit his head from the inside

And here comes the copter
Chop Chop Chop Chop Chop Chop Chop Chop

Spotlight
On him—

        one crip locked up
        one blood dead

Rewind to where—

        one young brother alive
        two young brothers alive
        three young brothers alive
        four young brothers unconfined

This is how you get out
Move to flows new
All slick

Move with books
Breaking types
Breaking norms of what it means
To be black
Breaking them side glances
Voices saying

*What
you think you white?*

And you see new paths to set ablaze

But
I'd burn it all
If it meant saving
One blood
One crip

THIS AMERICAN CONDITION

hold my tongue;
resist the urge.
find comfort
in blackness
in centuries of bold voices
in songs that celebrate rebellion.
I ease into furious sessions of writing.
I give this day my vision,
my funky insight;
ideas perform like enraged bass lines.
I keep playing out of sync.
This is flight.
This is freedom.
This is a human attempt
at mastering fate.
I am here—
a follower of the Most High,
a witness to conditions.

HATHAWAY

And so there it is
He sits hard on the curb waiting for the lean in
Barrel close
Cuffs tight
These conditions heavy
He's my brother
I hear you Donny
But he's heavy
They heavy
White police
Brown police
Black police
In between
They heavy Donny

STRANGE DNA

We forge our way into a narrative—
we created civilizations.
We are stone.
We are iron.
We are jazz.
We are resistant to the rules.
The laws govern farm animals.
The pigs are restless.
They are rich with green faces—
blood money.
We get down for freedom!
We dance for rights!
We sing to show our kinship with the sun.
We live.
We love.
We die.

Our heroes never
appear on stamps.

SAID ELEVEN TIMES
—for Eric Garner

I can't breathe
I can't breathe
I can't breathe
I can't breathe
I can't breathe
I can't breathe
I can't breathe
I can't breathe
I can't breathe
I can't breathe
I can't breathe

ON THE BLACK HAND SIDE

Daddy said defend the home,
protect the Queen,
fight for sister,
flash a middle finger,
brandish a crooked smile;

I still adhere to rituals,
routines,
dreams with snipers in clouds.
This is a subculture blueprint,
a means to function in chaos,
a strategy to arm voices.

Some say
Black Lives Matter
All Lives Matter
No Lives Matter.
I say draw a line in sand,
and be a frontline dreamer;
learn to disrupt the jungle,
learn to craft wings—birds aren't the only
ones with distant destinations.
I live for respect,
for surreal sun,
for a child's self-esteem,

for blaring music,
for the Creator's wide breath,
His broad salute,
Her motivating touch.

This place is a suite,
a place of safety,
a place of refuge.

I live on the black hand side.

NOT ENOUGH

out here tonight on the road trying to get home
to someone

the man who later will open his door
look into nothing before turning on the television to feel

and when that's not enough to
endure stillness

comes the second where
all that is left

is
the hum of existence

these matters of how we treat
blackness

SO CALLED LIFE

I burn.
I hustle.
I scramble for the ball.
I compose the solo—
Coltrane in '56.
Dead Prez rages in my veins.
I cheat the system.
I need the paper.
I need a fix—
that relaxing high,
that resistance in my soul.
Heaven is a home.
Heaven is a paradise.
I define my existence.
I celebrate heroes
with different colored flags
with different identities
with different convictions
that shake ground.
I talk jazz.
I talk hip hop.
I talk Africa.
I talk that liberation-funk.
I walk with ambition.
I walk with hostile B.P.M.

This is for country.
This is for polluted symbols.
This is for evolution.
I put in earbuds.
A skateboard clacks the street—kick,
push … coast   through ruins.

CHECK

if we could loosen up a bit
take off the mask

let go of fear bellowing in stomachs
to yell at stars and ask why

and it is that easy black man
easy when we silence the blood

inward killing
and walk tall towards it all

towards the source
all systems put in check

yes black man up
off the streets

and check-in on lamar
rock and chappelle

knowledge
dropped loud daily

WALK WITH A LIMP

Into the paint
into the abyss
into social dysfunction;
I tilt my crown,
I live,
I breathe.
Maya warned me about cages,
about circumstances,
about snakes in front yards.
Night is a friend,
a cousin itching to swing a fist,
to light a match,
to change the music,
to walk the path,
to provide an ear.
These days are mazes;
beauty is in my eye.
I whistle for protection,
but power is in the walk.

SANCHEZ: SONIA

black-white man swivel
in uneasiness   call on
me me me me me

MORRISON: JIM

i find god
in a desert,
expansive like the far corners
of the mind.

i recline and let divinity
circulate:
its swollen breath,
its surreal body,
its evolving presence.

on stage,
i surrender to an alternate reality;
the space is filled with
art,
poetry,
music;
a rebellious
beauty
is my natural home,
a liberated place
where angels sing
in a counterculture
tongue.

WHITE MEN

Some of them get it

Dylan
Kerr
Rapaport
Wise
Eggers
Ruffalo

Some
Like the line immortalized by singleton and spoke by cube

> *either they don't know, don't show, or don't care*
> *about what's going on in the hood*

FREE

Lost in social wilderness;
the traffic is heavy,
quick,
destructive.
Horns blare;
voices bounce off bumpers;
glances reflect in mirrors.
I fit the description,
but I don't care.
I don't stop.
I don't yield to racists
or cops,
or flags,
or Orange presidents,
or insecure men,
with Bibles swelling their chests.
I tumble through streets,
absorbing energy,
deflecting hate,
chasing dreams,
protecting the muse—
free.

COUNTERCULTURE TONE

smith took the podium in Mexico

black socks

     black folks in poverty

black scarf

     black pride

right hand
black glove
thrusted fist

carlos
norman
with him

     bless them

ashe
ali
understood

reid
kap
understand

AMERICAN REVERIE

I learn hate
from society's
wolves,
pigs,
and upright snakes.

I learn peace from men,
women,
children
that honor faith—

they look for stone
monuments to deface.

OLD MAN IN FRONT OF JOHNNY'S PASTRAMI STAND

Old man say sit down for a minute
Young buck what you about to do

Put a bullet in him
Him you   Listen youngster

See I did already done did what you about to do
Took a brother's life   took it right here

See I'm trying to teach you peace
But these streets   yo   ain't havin' it

So go on
Just know you ain't gotta do that

Shit
You got the barrel pointed in the wrong direction

GOOD GUYS WITH GUNS

Bullets pollute,
scatter,
break up lives,
pierce wings.
The police bring their guns,
their attitudes,
their disregard
for black skin.
I protect my flesh
with armed reason,
violent intellect,
a loud blues
on the forefront
of the American
condition.
I roll dice on frontlines,
smiling,
walking like a god,
ignoring the fact
that they are busily
adjusting their aims.

MUH TOLD ME TO SWING HARD

I was six. And I was small. White skin. Black heart. Don't
let nobody call you a white boy.

You hear me?

I was six. And I was small. White skin. Black heart. Black
mom. White dad. I was six.

Looking back. She knew. I swung hard. I swung often.

How I wish I was still that brave six-year-old. Life settles
you.

A MONSTER CALLED BREAST CANCER

A downward spiral.
The speed is akin to an uncontrolled
plunge into a medical Sunken Place.
We are a blues people.
We speak sun-words.
We didn't ask for this.
We didn't ask for this.
The Most High is too kind
to put His children in a condition,
too kind to put His lesser gods in
a fight to merely exist with
infections,
bacteria,
incessant beeps
in the night,
machines designed to keep
the body cool.
We are a blues people.
We speak sun-words.
We didn't ask for this.
We didn't ask for this.
I observe her struggle to breathe.
Her cough scares me, but the nurse
says *this* is progress.
This is a road to a solution,

to health,
to wellness.
My baby is a fighter.
My baby is a dreamer.
She's equipped to slay beasts.

'CAUSE THERE AIN'T NEVER BEEN A PEOPLE LIKE US

We sang
We sang
We sang
Our smiles
Our blues
We sang
We sang
We sang
Our smiles
Our blues
We sang
We sang
We sang
Our smiles
Our blues
We sang
We sang
We sang

GOLDEN DAYS FOR THE REST OF US

just need to stretch out.
These wings need a place
to be,
a place to rest,
a place to call paradise.
Somewhere down the street
a child looks for a better way,
a rationale gifted by the Creator.
His jeans are torn.
His spirit is low.
He still has a bop in his step.
His dreams perform a ritual,
like an artist approaches a canvas.
I identify with black boy magic,
with black girl essence,
with refugees fleeing conflict,
with hustlers in pool halls.
My eye is on the Cue ball.
My friend is the 8 ball.
I walk but I prefer to fly in
hostile circumstances.
Golden days are priceless.
Golden days are priceless.

I WALK BUT I PREFER TO FLY IN HOSTILE CIRCUMSTANCES

Fellow poet
My brother
I love you

I too believe in black boy magic and black girl essence

Fellow poet
My brother
I love you

I too love the hustle of the streets and them folks pounding
    pavement to cope

Fellow poet
My brother
I love you

I too believe in the rift of words is where it rests and spears
    loathing

Fellow poet
My brother
I love you

I too believe the fly in is imperative

DEATH OF ANOTHER RAPPER

The fat cats commercialized
black death.
Made it marketable.
Made it acceptable.
Made it cool.
Made it status quo
to strive
for scars
for bullets
for prison sentences
for status feeds
for threats
for wounds
for violent viral videos
for foreign cars
for misogyny
for abuse.
This system is old and archaic.
We gave them this steering wheel.
We structured this tradition.
They benefit from what we created
tolerated, and allowed to breathe.
Young boys want the fame and fortune,
but the price is heavy,
but the price is real.

They operate in fatal culture.
They run through landmines
for the chips
for the bag
for the scratch
for the paper.
Dead white men grin.
Dead white men know the value
of slave culture.
Another rapper leaves the earth.
The people mourn.
The people cry.
The people analyze,
trying to make sense of a puzzle.
His life mattered.
Black teens matter.
They laugh.
They scream.
They run up the hills.
They disappear.

WALKING THROUGH DOWNTOWN SAN JOSE
WITH CHRIS ABANI

Poet
Rapper
Writer

Us sipping warm coffee
Sharing an oral history of relationships formed
Finished and reinvented as they had to be

This sculpture of the Aztec god of wind and wisdom stops us
Name slipping us both until you say Quetzalcoatl
We pause

I tell you about my mother's lovely
Brutal times
You share how you sat with your brother in stillness

Our history coiled
Mothers white and black
Fathers black and white

These silent songs
I imagine in this silence
Caress us

We write them down as homage
To the ones
We love

CRISIS ON THE BORDER

Agents break up families
or criminals
or have-nots
or dreamers
or seekers of freedom
or people who love their skin
or people who love their sun.
God said welcome the foreigner,
but Americans see a threat to a polluted way of life.
This must be
the 1600s
the 1700s
the 1800s.
Pick a century and look for the blood.
Pick a century and look for genocide.
Pick a century when All Lives Mattered.
They think ideals erase
bloody history
racist history
backwards history.
A country has to look better
than its constitution
than its creed
than its currency.

I play a blues for my brother.
I play a blues for my sister.
I play a blues for children.

They used to separate us
and violate our women
and brutalize our men
and torment our children
and burn our towns.

Now identities have shifted.
Threat levels have changed.
The people cross the land.
The laws will never mean much
to the desperate
to the hungry
to those escaping hostility.
The people want wings,
like we want wings.
The people want to sing,
like we want to sing.
They tie their aspirations to the soil.
They secure their ambitions to
opportunities.
They plan to live
to breathe
to work
to love.

Walls will never be high enough
to keep out the beauty
the persistence
the longevity
of struggle.

CHUCK D

Close eyes
Feel these days of Trump
Clown

      Solace
      A rap blues
      In chest
      Voice
      Lyrics
      Unmistakable

Shut 'em down
Shut 'em down

Shut 'em
Shut 'em
Shut 'em

Shut 'em down
Shut 'em down

Shut 'em
Shut 'em

Shut 'em

We gotta Shut 'em down

FIGHT THE POWER

My father's mixes
taught me self-defense,
honor, and culture:
Long Beach in the 1980s
put wings on my back,
fuel in my stomach,
a gentle fire in the eyes.

Magic handled
the rock, ran the floor,
like a soldier on the field.
Kareem dropped the skyhook
and made me believe
in black eagles:
a song of resistance
played
in my head.

This was life for a dreamer,
a place where I kept snipers
in clouds and goals
on my skin.

CHOPPERS ON ADAMS BOULEVARD

LA in the 1980s
Kool & The Gang's Celebrate an anthem inside the walls of
    our home

Outside choppers
Race down Adams Boulevard on a purple blue sunset
    Sunday

This dream secure
Before night

When blades of LAPD choppers cut sky
Their spot beams white upside the canvas of our
    neighborhood

Looking for young
Brothers

While I watch Rod Carew
Hit a ball so smooth

Wishing I was somewhere else
But here

Inside these walls
Afraid of both the cops & my brothers

Both with
Choppers

AMERICAN REVERIE

WHAT'S IN A NAME?

In a name,
I see culture,
rebellion,
a grip on history.

I extend my fingertips
into the past,
to celebrate
a God they never
respected,
a journey they never
understood,
a thousand words for
the Creator that already
roamed the land.

On solemn wings
of music, resistance,
resilience,
and brutality,
I search for sky,
etch my initials on centuries
of expansive
canvas.

What's in a name besides
a frontline that steals
my time,
breath,
and energy?

Buried beneath it are martyrs
that I chant:
Trayvon Martin
Tamir Rice
Sandra Bland
Nia Wilson.

I sing for those who have not
been counted,
for the ones that took
titles to survive,
for the ones that jumped
from ships.

I honor people.
I honor stories.

In a name,
I see culture,
a grip on history,
a grip on history,
a

grip
on
history.

JABBAWOCKEEZ

The people tick and sway along highways of cities
An American hip-hop dance flow
That will not be stopped
Not as long as we have
Gaye and Terrell
Clinton and Mayfield
Lamar and Hill
Pulling us in synch
So when our faces tilt to stare at the murder
Murderer
How can you wonder
How can you face
How can you walk away
And not feel the rebellion comin'

BABY GIRL NEEDS ME TO PARK

rush through traffic
to handle
the business;
baby girl needs me to park
near a park,
where she can stretch her spirit,
like little, brown girls
like little, black angels
born on the other side
of the moon.
I hustle
because she depends
on my ambitions,
a soul brother,
an African brother—
my toenails have blackened
from walking cold,
American land.
I complete the tasks,
avoid the crosshairs;
police officers are dangerous
to my health.
Baby girl needs me
to park
near a park.

I fly because of love
and her mission
to live
to run
to be free.

THE OTHER DAY

My daughter backed the Prius out of the garage
A wave before the rev of the closing

She proud to be driving
Sixteen

And I can't remember it all
How the little girl up on my shoulders

Is now the young lady who writes about the importance of
Professional athletes using their public platform to speak out
    about injustice

Even though her English teacher smirked when notified of
    her topic
Oh you are writing about that

Turlock is not in the most progressive part of California
But the other day

My daughter
Mexican, Peruvian, African-American and Jewish

Backed the Prius out of the garage
A wave before the rev of the closing

Her spirit
Free

LISTEN, BREATHE, AND STRETCH WINGS

A breath is heavy.

God is expansive,
overwhelming,
a rhythm in feet,
a song vibrating
on concrete.

His riffs penetrate
the body, like Hendrix
saying hello
to my bones
to my dreams
to hostilities
burning through
veins.

I'm on a natural high,
walking on a cloud,
living for poems
of change
of resistance
of peace.

I celebrate vision,

freedom,
people
with big voices,
big hearts,
large identities:
they fly like dragons,
darting through sky,
cutting through tension.

I live, breathe,
stretch wings;
I'm just
an epic bard,
perfecting my yawp!

THÍCH QUẢNG ĐỨC

My brother your words bring the image of the soul who
    burned himself to death in Saigon.
Brother saying no to a government that shook to eliminate
    those like him. An act of defiance
Against an unjust government in 1963.

When we talk protest, death is the ultimate thrust. Thích
    Quảng Đức.
Brother Buddhist, and those with him in struggle, said
    enough.

I don't have that kind of courage.
If I'm real about it,
I blew up my marriage. And I
Clash today on how to be with a woman.

How does one be both black and white. Not a question. I
    live this.
I don't know how to be an ex-addict. If I'm honest, I'm so
    fragile I scare myself.
Yet, watching this monk lose himself in flames there are
    tears.
I am tired of drowning.

SOIL IN MY POCKETS

Cowardice climbs
along
the
spine
    of
             people that beat
on their chests.
They get emotional
when speech is free,
when freedom
is void of racism,
sexism,
and xenophobia.
I hustle for an armed
rationale.
I sing for have-nots
that may lose
their lives
in this concrete Hell,
in this hostile oblivion,
where snakes and devils
arrest you for crossing
the street,
sign laws that clip beautiful wings,
and kill

because some skin tones threaten
livelihoods
or brand blues
        on funky winds.

NEW TESTAMENT
—*for Jericho Brown*

All of it there
All of it
Our voices and words on beams of funk bright light Clinton
I hope you feel it in the words
In the P-Funk slices upside the head
Go back
Really hear
Franklin
Flack
Simone
Then
Go read Jericho Brown's *The New Testament*
All of it there
All of it

HEARTBEAT

Afraid
of
the
truth;
the youth
look
strange,
look mean,
look calm,
like
       bombs,
or lions,
ready to eat,
to roar,
to fly
across terrain
and then return home.
They protect flesh
and ideas;
they play for keeps
in the maze,
in the trap,
in the streets.
Their hearts beat
for memories

and loved ones.
They keep names
on lips—a unique way
to honor,
to celebrate,
to live.

BALTIMORE

and so I sit with you in space our
words colliding yet

gentle
inside the other's narrative

full and incomplete
sunflowers and lantanas around us all

BITTER TASTE

the bitter pill
of american blues
builds
my personality,
shapes my rough identity,
provides my temple
with the right nutrition
to defend itself.
Huey had it right in the '60s.
Ida B. Wells had   it
                        right
in
the 1890s.
I have a right to prepare
nooses
for system malfunction
for a flag with my ancestors' screams
echoing
building
climbing
peaks
into high-pitched oblivion
where apple pies
cut the lips
the tongue.

razorblades taste like freedom
                    like grace
                    like baptism
by western expansion.
I talk to Yeshua,
like dreadlocks crawl from His scalp.
this riff whispers to the Most
High: my belly
          is
          full.

Do you hear me, do you feel me? We gon' be alright

—Kendrick Lamar

ACKNOWLEDGMENTS

I would like to acknowledge the poets, writers, artists, and activists who have given me the courage to approach poetry with humility, urgency, and righteous anger. May the poems in this book inspire, educate, enlighten, and disrupt.

"This American Condition" and "Free" originally appeared on the recording *Vibes and Laps, Vol. 1.*

"A Monster Called Breast Cancer" originally appeared in *Dissident Voice*.

—SL

"Hathaway" originally appeared in the *Free Slang Poetry Review.*

"Walking Through Downtown San Jose with Chris Abani" originally appeared in *Nomad's Choir Poetry Journal.*

"The Other Day" and "Thích Quảng Đức" originally appeared in *Penumbra*.

All love/peace/thanks to TDM.

—DM

ABOUT THE AUTHORS

Synnika Alekzander-Chizoba Lofton is an award winning poet, educator, and recording artist. Lofton is the author of seventeen books and more than 150 spoken word albums and singles. He is a Literature instructor at Chesapeake Bay Academy and a lecturer at Norfolk State University.

Donnelle McGee is the author of *Ghost Man*, a novel (Sibling Rivalry Press); *Shine*, a novella (Sibling Rivalry Press); and *Naked*, a collection of poetry (Unbound Content). He earned his MFA from Goddard College. He is a faculty member at Mission College in Santa Clara, California. His work has appeared in *Controlled Burn, Colere, Haight Ashbury Literary Journal, Home Planet News, Iodine Poetry Journal, Permafrost, River Oak Review, The Spoon River Poetry Review,* and *Willard & Maple*, among others. He is the founder and publisher of Thera Books, and he also serves as the Lead Poetry Editor for *Clockhouse*. His work has been nominated for a Pushcart Prize.

ABOUT THE PRESS

Thera Books is an independent publishing house based in Turlock, California. We aim to publish writers pushing the boundaries of literature and writing about what it means to be human.

www.thetherabooks.com